Contents

D0313643

Acknowledgements
Photographs on front and back cover, inside back cover and pages 21 and 37 courtesy of Empics Ltd. Photographs on inside front cover and pages 2, 8, 13, 19, 38 and 44 courtesy of Getty Images. Photographs on pages 41 and 43 courtesy of BISI. All other photographs courtesy of Louis Ross.
Diagrams by Margaret Jones.

Note Throughout the book players are referred to individually as 'he'. This should, of course, be taken to mean 'he or she' where appropriate.

A short history

It is known that around 1860, the daughters of the Duke of Beaufort were playing Battledore and Shuttlecock in the great hall of Badminton House, the seat of the Somerset family in Gloucestershire, England. To add a little variety, they rigged up a string across the hall from the doorway to the fireplace and the aim of the game was to try to keep the shuttle going by playing it to each other over the string. It is believed that Mr J. L. Baldwin suggested that it would be more amusing if the shuttle were to be hit away from instead of towards players on the other side of the string. The sport of badminton had been created.

By the mid to late 1870s indoor clubs were being formed in England and in no time at all clubs were wishing to pit their skills against each other. It is interesting to note that there were no shuttlecock manufacturers in those days, so players had to make their own shuttlecocks from whatever materials were available. Until 1893, when the forerunner of the Badminton Association of England was formed, there were no laws governing the size of court dimensions, numbers of players or scoring.

Since then badminton has developed into a true sport for all. It can be played by men or women, young or old, and it is also thriving in sporting competitions for the disabled. Size or strength give no particular advantage: it is a game of technical and tactical skill which at international level demands high levels of fitness. Badminton is one of the few sports in which a woman can compete on equal terms in a partnership with a man; indeed, mixed doubles is regarded as one of the most entertaining forms of badminton.

The game

The game of badminton is played on a court by two players (singles) or four players (doubles). The players use rackets to hit a shuttle over a net from one side to the other, the object of the game being to hit the shuttle across the net to a place on the opponent's court where he cannot reach it, or to force the opponent to hit the shuttle out of court or into the net. A player who achieves this when he or his partner has served is awarded a point, and the first player or pair to reach the required number of points in a game wins that game. A match is the best of three games.

Because of the extreme lightness of the shuttle, which is affected by the slightest breeze, the game is largely played indoors.

Badminton has far outgrown its origins and is now generally rated, in its higher grades, as one of the fastest and most exhausting pursuits in the athletic world. The initial velocity which can be imparted to the shuttle by good racket work, and the fact that the shuttle must not hit the floor, are the principal reasons for this. It follows that there can be no better means for attaining perfect physical fitness, and that really good footwork is essential for success.

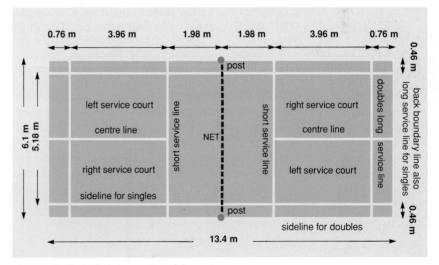

▲ *Fig. 1 The badminton court and dimensions*

The court

Dimensions of the court are shown in fig. 1 on page 3. The surfaces of the court should be of wood, although other surfaces may serve equally well, provided they are not slippery. Because the shuttle is white in colour, the floor and background should be of a dark shade, and if painted should not be glossy, as reflection makes sighting of the shuttle difficult. The court markings must be clearly defined, preferably by white or yellow lines. These lines should be 40 mm wide; they indicate the boundaries of the various areas of the court as shown in the diagram. All lines form part of the area which they define.

The dimensions of the net are shown in fig. 2 and the net posts must be placed on the outer sidelines, with no intrusion onto the court, or sunk into the court on the outside line. There should be no gaps between the ends of the net and the posts.

In cases where it is impracticable to fix the posts to the floor, it is accepted practice to fasten the net rope to the walls of the room. If this is done, a tape of 40 mm in width should be fixed to the top of the net and the floor exactly over the outer sidelines to indicate where the posts should be, as shown in fig. 3 on page 5.

Sometimes communal posts are used for adjacent courts, being placed between the courts. In this case also, tapes should be fixed over the outer sidelines of both courts.

The posts themselves should not be higher than 1.55 m. This is important, as, by their position on the sidelines, they actually stand within the playing area. Apart from the type which screw on to the floor, posts can also be obtained which will remain erect by means of a weighted base.

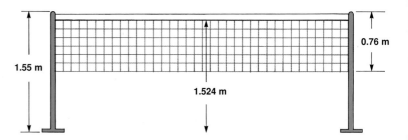

▶ *Fig. 2 Net dimensions*

Service areas

The service areas are those areas in which a player must stand to serve – either in the right or the left service area – and also the areas in which the receiver must stand until after the service is delivered.

A foot on or touching a line in the case of either the server or the receiver is held to be outside the service court and therefore is a fault.

The areas are as indicated in figs 4 and 5. The centre line dividing the right and left areas is regarded as 'in court' for either side should the shuttle fall on that line.

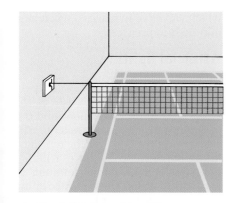

▲ *Fig. 3 Net fastened to walls*

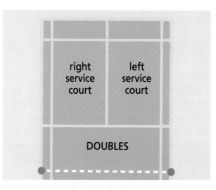

▲ *Fig. 4 Doubles service areas*

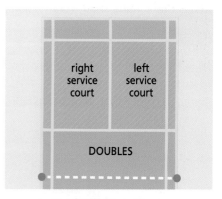

▲ *Fig. 5 Singles service areas*

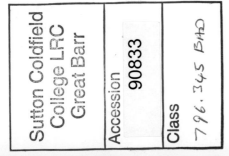
5

A suitable hall

The height of the hall should be 7.6 m for a Development Centre, and 9.1 m for a Performance and Development Centre, over the whole area of the court. A hall with a slightly lower roof can be used, but it would not be suitable for first class play. The area around the court between the baseline and the wall should be a minimum of 2.5 m; and 2.3 m between the side line and the wall.

The background should be uniform in colour. The walls should be finished in medium to dark shades with a matt surface. The floor finish should be dull, not glossy or shiny or slippery. The marking lines should, preferably, be white, but may be yellow if this helps to distinguish them from those used for other sports.

When the court is permanently in use for badminton the best posts to use are those with a metal base which can be screwed to the floor. Alternatively, posts can be obtained with well weighted bases which will hold the net taut at the correct height.

Daylight

The daylight, if any, should come from above, through skylights on the north or east side to avoid sun glare. If windows are necessary for other reasons, then they must have curtains or blinds which can be drawn across when badminton is in progress.

Artificial lighting

Good light is provided by two groups of lamps positioned on each side of the court, 4.88 m from the floor and 0.6 to 0.9 m outside, and parallel to, the sidelines centralised over the net. Each fitting should, ideally, have a line of tungsten opaque lamps totalling at least 1,000 watts. These may be either hung from the roof or fixed to posts.

A fully detailed pamphlet on halls suitable for badminton is available from the Badminton Association of England (*see* address on page 45).

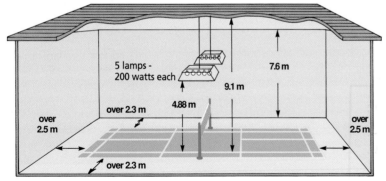

5 lamps -
200 watts each

7.6 m

9.1 m

4.88 m

over
2.3 m

over
2.5 m

over
2.5 m

over 2.3 m

▲ *Fig. 6 Badminton hall*

6

Equipment

The racket

Modern badminton rackets can weigh less than 100 g, which obviously enables them to be moved and 'thrown' with tremendous speed. Recent tests have shown that the shuttle can leave the racket at over 200 miles per hour. Most rackets are now of a one-piece graphite construction, which has made the metal-head racket almost obsolete. There have also been developments in the shape of the racket, with the head being extended down to form a 'V' shape at the shaft. This increases the 'sweet spot' of the racket. With such a variety of rackets now available, at a wide range of prices, it is important to test as many as possible before purchasing.

The shuttle

Two basic types are available: feathered or synthetic. The feathered shuttle is very fragile, weighing only 4.74–5.5 g, and it is more expensive than the synthetic type. It is made from 16 goose feathers inserted in a cork base, the base being covered with kid. Being fragile, it should be treated with great care and never hit along the floor. Once the feathers become damaged, the flight will be affected.

Because of the different atmospheric conditions of different halls and weather, shuttles are made in varying speeds and Law 4 will help in ascertaining the correct speed for any condition. It states that 'A shuttle shall be deemed to be of correct pace when it is hit by a player with a full underhand stroke from a spot immediately above one back boundary line in a direction parallel to the sidelines and at an upward angle, to fall not less than 530 mm and not more than 990 mm short of the other back boundary line.'

In a very clear atmosphere a shuttle will travel further than on a misty day, and likewise the size and temperature of a hall will affect the flight of the shuttle.

Synthetic shuttles have been approved for play in many places and can be obtained in various speeds. A skirt of synthetic material replaces the natural feathers and the base may also be of synthetic material. Compared with feathered shuttles they are more durable, reasonably inexpensive and thus widely used by beginners and average club players.

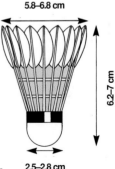

▶ *Fig. 7 Shuttle dimensions*

Dress

Although dress is largely a matter of personal choice, there are two important considerations. Because badminton is a fast game, freedom of movement is essential. Clothing worn on court, therefore, must always be comfortable and must stay comfortable throughout the game.

Shorts and shirt are the normal clothes for the players and very often a track suit is worn off court.

Badminton is often played in inadequately heated halls and it is usually advisable, under these conditions, to wear warm clothing when knocking-up and starting the game.

Special attention should be paid to footwear, as uncomfortable shoes will undoubtedly hamper performance. Shoes should be cushioned and should not have black soles. They are usually worn with thick socks to prevent feet blistering.

The doubles game

The doubles game is the most common in badminton. Before the game is commenced, the sides 'toss'. This is usually done by one member of a side spinning the racket and one of the opposing side calling 'rough' or 'smooth' – this refers to the way the stringing appears at the throat of the racket as it falls. Alternatively, the shuttle may be struck in the air and whichever side of the net the base points that pair has the choice of deciding (a) to serve first, or (b) not to serve first, or (c) which side of the court to commence play. The side losing the toss has a choice of the remaining alternatives.

In a match played over the best of three games the side winning the previous game will serve first in the proceeding game.

The pair delivering the opening service decides which player shall serve, and similarly the receiving pair decides which player will receive the first service.

The pair serving is referred to as the 'in' side and the pair receiving, the 'out' side.

The first service must be delivered from the right-hand service court and directed to the diagonally opposite court, i.e. the receiver's right-hand court, as shown in fig. 8 (right).

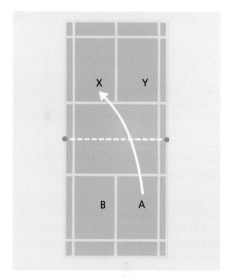

▲ *Fig. 8 First service*

9

Service

To make a correct service a player must:

- wait until the receiver is ready (however, neither side may cause undue delay to the delivery of the service)
- stand within the limits of his own service court (right or left according to his score)
- have some part of both feet stationary on the ground until the service is delivered
- ensure that the shuttle at the instant of being struck is below the waist
- ensure that all the head of the racket at the instant of striking the shuttle is below any part of the hand holding the racket
- hit the shuttle directly over the net into the service court diagonally opposite
- ensure a continuous forward movement after the start of the service until the service is delivered
- ensure the initial point of contact with the shuttle is on the base of the shuttle, i.e. not on the feathers.

The server must not make any feint with the intention of deceiving or baulking his opponent before or during the service.

If the server commits a fault, he loses the service.

▲ *Preparing to serve*

Service faults

The following photographs show common faults in delivering service.

▲   *Ensure that all the head of the racket, at the instant of striking the shuttle, is below any part of the hand holding the racket*

◀   *Ensure that the shuttle, at the instant of being struck, is below the waist*

Order of service

Assume A and B are playing against X and Y. A and B win the toss and A decides to serve. X decides to receive. A serves from the right-hand court to X in his right-hand court. If A's side wins the opening rally they will score a point, and the same server will serve again, this time from the left court to Y in his left court.

A will go on serving alternately from each service court to each opponent in turn until his side loses a rally. When that happens, the service passes to the other side, XY, and the player in the right service court will serve to the opponent who, at the beginning of the previous rally, was in his right service court.

This same player will continue to serve, alternately from each service court, until his side loses a rally, at the same time adding to his side's score every time they win a rally. When he loses a rally he loses the right to continue to serve and it will be the turn of his partner to commence his innings. This player will start serving from the service court in which he was standing at the beginning of the previous rally.

Thus, each partner will have an innings in turn, and when both partners have lost the right to continue to serve, the service will again pass to the opponents, the one in the right service court commencing. It will be noted that the only time when this does not happen is at the very beginning of a game, when only one of the two partners has an innings.

Receiving the service

The receiver must stand within the limits of the service court diagonally opposite to the server. His feet must be entirely within the lines marking the boundary of the court, and must not touch them. As with the server, one part of both feet must remain stationary on the ground until the service is delivered. His actual position depends on personal choice, but he should stand as near as he can to the short service line to be able to 'kill' a short service, but still be able to get back to a deep high service. If the receiver thinks the service will not fall within his court he will allow the shuttle to hit the floor. If his judgement is correct the service is a fault. Should the shuttle fall within the court, or on the surrounding lines, the serve is good and the server wins a point.

As soon as the service has been delivered, players may move to any position for subsequent shots, the only restriction being that a player may not cross into his opponent's half of the court.

▲ *Receiving service in the doubles game*

Scoring

Only the side which is at the time serving may add to its score, that is, when the server's side wins a rally they score a point, whereas if the opponents win that particular rally they do not score a point; instead, they have the satisfaction of causing the server to lose the right to serve. When both partners have lost the right to serve, then, as already explained, the service will pass to the other side which then has the opportunity of adding to their score.

Scoring in a typical game is illustrated by the diagrams on page 15. AB are playing XY. AB win the toss and decide to serve. A delivers the service and X decides to receive.

● Fig. 9: A serves from the right-hand court to X in his right-hand court. AB win the rally. The score is one-love.
● In fig. 10, A serves from the left-hand court to Y in his left-hand court. AB win the rally. The score is two-love.

● Next (fig. 11), where A serves from the right-hand court to X in his right-hand court. XY win the rally.
● Service passes to XY. The score is love-two (the server's score is called first). X, being in the right-hand court, takes the service and serves to A who was in his right-hand court at the commencement of the last rally (fig. 12). XY win the rally. The score is one-two.
● X now serves from the opposite court to B (fig. 13). AB win the rally. X loses the right to serve and Y delivers the next service. The score is one-two (second server).
● Y serves from the right-hand court, i.e. the court he was in at the beginning of the last rally, to A (fig. 14). AB win the rally. Y loses his service, XY lose the right to serve and AB take the service. The score is two-one.

● A in the right-hand court will serve. He serves until AB lose a rally, then the service passes to B.

In doubles and men's singles, a game is won by the first side to score 15 points, or 11 points in ladies' singles. If the score is 14 all (10 all in ladies' singles), the side which first scored 14 (10) shall exercise the following choice:

● to continue the game to 15 (11) points, or
● to 'set' the game to 17 (13) points (*see* page 18).

A match is normally the best of three games. Players should change ends at the completion of the first game, prior to the beginning of the third game (if any), and in the third game when the leading score reaches 6 in a game of 11 points, or 8 in a game of 15 points.

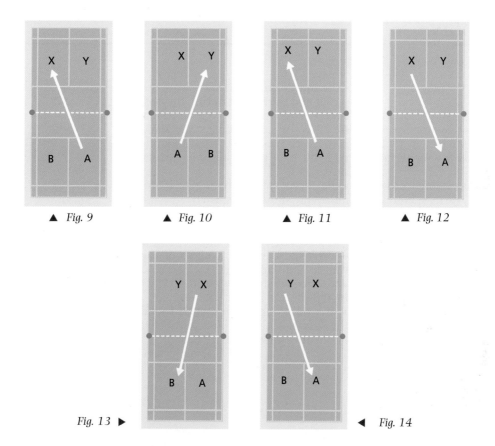

▲ *Fig. 9*　　　　▲ *Fig. 10*　　　　▲ *Fig. 11*　　　　▲ *Fig. 12*

Fig. 13 ▶　　　　◀ *Fig. 14*

Faults in play

A player's side loses the rally if:

• he fails to return the shuttle over the net into his opponent's court
• when the shuttle is in play, he touches the net or its supports with his racket, person or dress
• he strikes the shuttle before it crosses to his side of the net. He may, however, follow the shuttle over the net with his racket in the course of his stroke
• he touches the shuttle with his person or dress
• he obstructs an opponent, for instance sliding under the net, throwing a racket into an opponent's court, baulking or unsighting an opponent during service

• the shuttle is caught and held on the racket and then slung during the execution of a stroke; or if the shuttle is hit twice in succession by the same player with two strokes; or if the shuttle is hit by a player and his partner successively
• the server, in attempting to serve, misses the shuttle completely.

It is **not** a fault:

• to hit the base and feathers of the shuttle simultaneously
• to strike the shuttle with one distinct hit only by any part of the racket
• in a rally, to play the shuttle round the outside of the net post, provided it falls within the opponent's court.

▲ *Fig. 15 A shuttle falling on the line is 'in court' and must fall clear of the line bounding the court to be 'out of court'*

Lets

The only occasion when a rally may be held up without one side or the other winning it, is when a 'let' is granted.

▼ *Fig. 16 Formerly a service let, but since 1958 a good service*

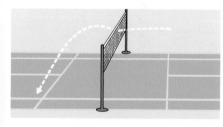

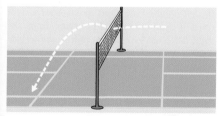

Lets in play

A let may be claimed when there is an accidental interference during play, such as a shuttle from an adjacent court invading the court, or if the shuttle in play should by some chance get caught in the net after passing over it.

A let may also be claimed: (a) by the receiver, if the server should serve from the wrong service court and win the rally; (b) by the server, should the receivers have changed courts and won the rally.

The above two lets may only be claimed immediately the rally has taken place. If such changes have occurred previously without notice, a let cannot be claimed and the faulting side continues to adhere to its present or 'wrong' service courts.

◄ *Fig. 17 Service fault*

Service lets

Service lets were abolished in 1958 so that, even if a shuttle in service touches the top of the net, the stroke is not thereby invalidated.

Note It is a fault if the shuttle, in service, strikes the net on its way across, but falls short of the short service line.

17

Setting

The singles game

When the score is level near the end of a game, so that each side requires only one point to win, the side which first reaches that score has the option of setting the game. When a game is set, it is won by the side which first reaches 17 points (13 points in ladies' singles).

For example, in the case of AB v XY, AB may be leading by 14 points to 11 in a 15-point game when XY regain the service and from their service win the next 3 points, bringing the score to 14 points all. Both sides now require 1 point to win the game. AB, being the first side to reach 14 points, have the option of setting the game. AB opt to set and the first side to reach 17 (13) points wins the game.

All the foregoing remarks apply to the singles game, with two important exceptions.

The first is the area of the service court. The 'tramlines' are not used at all for singles, the court thus being 1 m narrower. To compensate for the inability to use this area for serving, the service court in singles is extended to the baseline. A service may thus be hit to the very back of the court.

The second is that, in singles, a side can of course have only one innings, and in order to provide for the service to be delivered from the left court as well as from the right, the laws direct that the server shall serve from the right-hand service court when his particular score is '0' or any even number, and from the left-hand service court when his score is an odd number. Thus the service must be delivered from the court appropriate to the server's score.

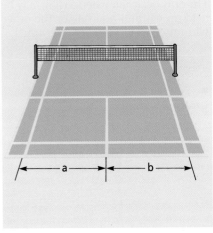

▲ *Fig. 18 Singles service: (a) serving from the left-hand service court to left-hand service court – score is odd; (b) serving from the right-hand service court to right-hand service court – score is 0 or even*

The strokes

Grip

Forehand

To work out the forehand grip, first hold the racket with your free hand by the shaft in front of you. Then spread the palm of your racket hand flat against the strings and move your hand down the shaft towards the handle. Gently curl your thumb and fingers around the handle so that the thumb and forefinger form a 'V' shape.

It is essential that the racket is held in a relaxed manner and is not grasped tightly in the palm of the hand.

Backhand

Holding the racket in the forehand grip, turn the racket slightly to the right (for right-handed players) or slightly to the left (for left-handed players) so that the thumb is on the flat side of the handle and can be used to give leverage.

▲ *Forehand grip*

▲ *Backhand grip*

The service

There are basically two serves: the low and the high. However, in the case of the high there are a couple of variations, the flick and the drive. The purpose of the low serve is to deliver the shuttle in such a way that it skims the top of the net, thereby allowing the opponent no opportunity to attack it by hitting it in a downward direction. The purpose of the high serve is to move the opponent to the rear of the court.

The short serve

The short serve should skim the top of the net and should land just inside the service line of the receiver's court, thereby denying the opponent the chance to attack. It may be played with a forehand or a backhand stroke.

Forehand short service

• Preparation
The stance should be easy, with the weight balanced between the feet and the non-racket foot forwards. The shuttle is held out in front of the body, with the racket back, the arm bent at the elbow and the wrist held back.

• Just after release of the shuttle
The shuttle is released and the racket is brought forwards as the weight is transferred on to the forward foot. Note that the wrist is held back and the eyes are watching the shuttle.

• At impact
The wrist is still held back, the weight is on the front foot and the eyes are still watching the shuttle.

• After impact
The wrist continues to be held back.

• Follow through
The racket is at the limit of its travel, the wrist is still held back and the eyes follow the flight of the shuttle.

Common faults
Beginners tend to hold the shuttle too far to the side of the body, take an excessive backswing and use the wrist in the hitting action. These factors lead to loss of control and the shuttle travelling high above the net.

▲ *Forehand short service: preparation*

Backhand short service

A backhand service is achieved quite easily by most players and is an excellent service for the doubles game. Stand comfortably facing the net and well up to the front service line, with your feet astride or one foot forward as preferred. Hold the shuttle out in front of you, below your waist. Using a normal backhand grip (thumb down flat on the handle), hold the racket in front of your body, with your elbow well up. Make a short backswing from the elbow and strike the shuttle almost out of the hand holding it. Keep your eyes on the shuttle until it is struck.

- **Preparation**

The weight is balanced, with the feet astride or one foot forward. The shuttle is held well in front, below the waist. Using a backhand grip, the racket is held in front of the body and the elbow well up.

- **Backswing**

A short backswing is taken from the elbow.

- **Immediately after impact**

Strike the base of the shuttle, almost out of the hand holding it. Keep your eyes on the shuttle. *Note* The motion must be continuous.

- **Follow through**

The racket moves to the limit of its travel, and the eyes lift to follow the shuttle and to watch for the opponent's reaction.

Common faults

Beginners tend to hold the racket and shuttle too close to the body, which prevents a long enough backswing being taken. They also fail to lift the elbow high enough, which means the backswing does not begin from the elbow and they hit using only a wrist action.

▲ *Backhand short service: immediately after impact*

The long serve

Flick and drive serves

In the forehand and backhand short services, the wrist is held firm. In the flick and drive serves, on the other hand, the shuttle is literally flicked or driven to the rear of the court using a slight change to the service action to deceive the opponent. This is achieved by a last moment tightening of the grip and a quick 'flick' of the wrist to increase the speed of the racket head, thereby sending the shuttle quickly over the opponent's racket to the rear of the court. These two serves are used mainly in level and mixed doubles (*see* Tactics).

The high serve

The high serve is used mainly in singles. The shuttle is struck as high as possible to land as near the back line of the court as possible.

● **Preparation**
The feet, one behind the other, are shoulder width apart. Note that the wrist is held back. The shuttle is held at a full arm's length in front of the body – a large backswing is necessary to reach it. The eyes are focused on the shuttle.

● **At impact**
The weight has been transferred to the forward foot and the shuttle has been released from the hand. A full racket swing is made underneath the shuttle and the shuttle is then hit forwards and upwards. The eyes continue to focus on it.

● **After impact**
There is a full follow through of the racket and the eyes focus on the flight of the shuttle.

Common faults
Beginners tend to swing across, rather than straight through and underneath, the shuttle. This is often the result of holding the shuttle too close to or too far from the side of the body. They are also prone to cutting short the follow through and leaning backwards, which does not allow the weight to move through to the front foot. This causes the shuttle to go high but short of the back line.

▲ *High serve: preparation*

▲ *High serve: just before impact*

▶ *High serve: follow through*

Overhead strokes

Forehand overhead clear

This shot is used mainly in singles to push an opponent into the rear of the court and so create space in the forecourt. When it is hit very high (a defensive clear), it creates time for a player to recover to a central position. When it is hit flatter (an attacking clear), it makes an opponent move quickly from the forecourt to the rear court.

The techniques for all the overhead shots are very similar. The shuttle should be struck with a throwing action.

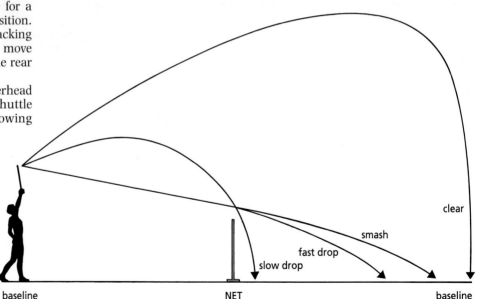

▼ *Fig. 19 Line of shuttle's flight with overhead strokes*

clear

smash

fast drop

slow drop

baseline   NET   baseline

● Preparation

The body should be positioned behind the shuttle, with the weight balanced between the feet. The elbow is bent.

● Before impact

The racket is dropped back behind the body. This is possible because of a relaxed grip on the racket and a 'loose' wrist. The eyes are focused on the shuttle, and the free arm and shoulder are pointing towards it. The weight is beginning to be transferred on to the front foot.

● At impact

The base of the shuttle is struck from almost directly above the head. Note that the racket has been thrown upwards, with the point of contact being as high as possible. Now the weight has been fully transferred on to the front foot and the shoulders are parallel to the net.

● After impact

The racket follows through along the intended direction of the shuttle and then down across the body.

Common faults

Players may not get their body behind the shuttle and they therefore are forced to strike it when it is actually behind them: rather than transferring their weight forwards into the stroke, their movement will be backwards after striking the shuttle. This will lead to a lack of power and direction. Another problem occurs when the shoulders stay parallel to the net, which is usually associated with a bent arm and a faulty grip.

▲ *Forehand overhead clear: impact*

▲ *Forehand overhead clear: preparation*

▲ *Forehand overhead clear: just before impact*

▲ *Forehand overhead clear: follow through*

Forehand smash

The smash is the main attacking stroke in badminton and the aim is to strike the shuttle downwards as quickly as possible on to the floor of the opponent's court. This is achieved by using exactly the same technique as that for the clear, except that the point of impact should be forwards of the head, which will cause the shuttle to travel downwards.

Common faults
Once again, not getting behind the shuttle is usually the main problem. However, players also tend to grip the racket too tightly when trying to smash, the result of which is a restriction in wrist movement and a reduction of power.

▲ *Forehand smash: just before impact*

29

Overhead drop shot

The aim here is to deceive an opponent. The preparation is the same as that for the clear and smash, but the momentum of the racket head is checked at the point of impact. This produces an unexpected slow shot which should land just beyond the net.

Common faults
Some players tend to alter their hitting movement and favour a 'patting' action rather than a full swing. The deception is therefore lost: the inception is lower and later, and the follow through is restricted.

▲ *Overhead drop shot: preparation*

▲ *Overhead drop shot: just after impact*

▲ *Straight drop shot: impact*

▲ *Cross-court drop shot: follow through*

Backhand overhead clear

Whenever possible, players should try to move across the court to play overhead shots on the forehand. However, there will be occasions when this is not feasible, so the backhand overhead clear is an essential stroke that allows time in which to recover position.

● **Preparation**
The back is turned towards the opponent's court, with the weight on the racket foot. The racket is held across the body with the backhand grip. The eyes focus on the shuttle over the racket.

● **Just before impact**
The racket travels from a low to a high position, with the wrist held back and about to straighten for impact, which should be high and to the side of the body.

● **At impact**
The wrist and forearm are 'flicked' at the shuttle. The eyes follow the shuttle's flight and the body is encouraged to turn back and face the net.

Common faults
Players may be guilty of throwing themselves at this stroke and swiping at the shuttle. This makes it very difficult to time the shot and gives little chance of directing the shuttle accurately. To correct the fault, concentrate on playing the stroke from a solid base, with both feet placed on the floor and the racket travelling from a low position across the body to a high position at impact.

▲ *Backhand overhead clear: preparation*

▲ *Backhand overhead clear: just before impact*

▲ *Backhand overhead clear: follow through*

33

Underarm strokes

Forehand and backhand underarm lifts

The underarm lift is a defensive stroke which is usually used when a player is in difficulty close to the net.

The weight is on the forward-facing racket foot and the racket is pointing towards the net. The racket is swung under the shuttle with a good follow through in an upward direction to give the shuttle maximum height and depth.

The backhand underarm lift involves exactly the same technique as that employed for the forehand, except of course that a backhand grip is adopted.

▲ *Forehand underarm lift*

Forehand and backhand drives

These are useful strokes to execute from the mid-court when the shuttle is too low to smash. They are used extensively by the man in mixed doubles. The aim is to drive the shuttle hard and flat over the net to limit the opposition's chance of attack.

Common faults
Players often throw themselves into this shot, causing loss of direction and control. The drive should be played from a solid base with a short, sharp strike of the shuttle to give maximum control and power with minimum effort.

▲   *Forehand drive*

Net shots

The essential point to remember with all net shots is that the shuttle should be struck as early as possible. It should also be struck from above net height in a downward direction in order to 'kill' it.

When the shuttle cannot be taken from above the net, an accurate net shot can be produced by using a relaxed and flexible backhand or forehand grip, as appropriate, and pushing the racket to the shuttle as early and as high as possible.

Common faults
Some players may attempt to play this shot with a stiff arm and a tight grip, which tends to cause the shuttle to bounce off the racket and so travel too high over the net.

▲ *Forehand net shot*

Receiving service

When receiving service it is important to have both knees flexed, with the non-racket foot forwards and the racket in front of the body at, or slightly above, net height. This position should enable the receiver to react quickly in an attacking manner to high or low services.

Common faults
Sometimes players stand in an upright position and keep the racket leg straight. This makes it very difficult for them to move quickly to the service, and so the shuttle is taken late and the opportunity to attack is lost.

Those players who do adopt an aggressive stance may subsequently fail to make the most of it, purely by hitting the shuttle and then letting their racket drop. With the racket below net height, it becomes impossible to play an attacking downward shot.

▲ *Receiving service*

Tactics

Singles

Since the singles court has more depth than width, clears and drops to the rear and forecourt are the shots to manoeuvre the opponent around it with a view to forcing errors or creating open space to play the quicker smash. When playing any shot in singles it is important to try to return to a central base position in the mid-court from where all possible replies can be covered. However, movement towards this base position should be 'checked' as the opponent makes his shot in order to avoid being wrong-footed. When in difficult situations the shuttle should be cleared as high as possible to the rear court to allow time to recover to base.

While playing the early stages of a game, attention should be paid to the opponent's strengths and weaknesses. For example, some players' backhand is often weaker than their forehand, so the fast clear, just high enough to avoid an early interception, may produce a weak return and create open space down their forehand side. So, always employ a strategy that exploits your opponent's weaknesses and try to keep the play *away* from his strengths.

To use any of these tactics, good stroke production and accuracy are essential, and the way to achieve these is through regular practice.

Doubles

Level doubles

The basic service is the low one. The server should follow it to the net to cover any replies and to force the receiver to lift the return to the server's partner in the rear court. High serves are used for variety and, since the receiver will have a chance to hit downwards, the server should retreat for defence to a position that is level with his partner in the mid-court.

The same system should be applied during rallies: if you or your partner lift the shuttle so that it can be hit downwards by your opponents, then adopt the side-by-side defensive formation; if, on the other hand, the shuttle is above net height, it should be hit downwards and the front and back formation adopted.

When using the former defensive formation, the aim is to play shots that the opposition will not be able to attack. These are usually drives through the front player or net shots in front of him. When a shot like this is attempted, as soon as the shuttle reaches a position on the opponent's side from where it cannot be attacked (i.e. at or below net height), the striker should immediately move in towards the net. This converts a defensive position into an attacking one. When the conversion shots are not feasible, the shuttle should be lifted deep to the rear of the court to allow time in which to cover the next shot.

In this attacking formation the rear court player should keep hitting downwards in a straight direction so that his partner knows roughly where the shuttle will be played. He should also use a variety of pace and angles to try to produce a weak reply for his partner. Only under exceptional pressure should the shuttle be lifted, because his partner at the net will be an easy target to attack.

The net player should be looking to intercept any replies that pass within reach. The racket must be kept above net height so that the shuttle can be taken as early as possible. If the shuttle cannot be 'killed', then it should be played tight to the net to force the opposition to lift it again, thereby maintaining the attack.

When attacking, cross-court shots should be played only occasionally, as they put the partner out of position and create space for the opposition to exploit.

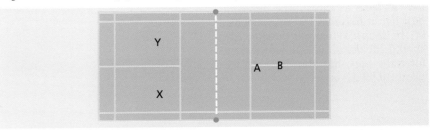

▲ *Fig. 20* '*Side-by-side*' *defensive formation* (left) *and* '*back-and-front*' *attacking formation* (right) *in doubles*

Mixed

The basic formation for mixed doubles involves the woman covering the forecourt and the man covering the mid- and rear court areas. To help assume this position, the woman should stand in front of the man, on his non-racket side, when he is serving.

As with level doubles, the low service is favoured, although a variety of high serves may be used frequently to the woman in an attempt to force her away from her forecourt position.

The role of the woman is similar to that of the net player in level doubles, i.e. she must stand in the forecourt, with her racket up and ready to intercept any shot she can take in front of her (as soon as the shuttle has gone past her, it becomes the responsibility of the man). Whenever possible, she should hit the shuttle downwards to force the opposing man to reach forwards to lift it.

The man's main objective should be to take the shuttle as early as possible and to strike it downwards or at least flat to prevent the opposition from attacking his partner. He must also avoid lifting it, as his partner at the net will have little time in which to react to a shuttle struck down at her. When a pair is forced to lift, the woman should always position herself across the court from where the opposition are hitting. This will give her slightly more time to sight the shuttle, since it will have a greater distance to travel to reach her.

Warm-up

When played competitively, badminton is a very strenuous game. It is therefore important to ensure that your body is properly prepared before you start any practice or game. To achieve this you need to go through a series of exercises, including jogging or skipping, that will both help to raise your pulse rate and to stretch the major muscle groups. Proper preparation will reduce the risk of sprains and strains which may occur when cold ligaments are subjected to sudden violent activities.

Badminton Into Schools Initiative

The Badminton Into Schools Initiative (BISI) has been created by the Badminton Association of England (BAofE). It is designed to cover all the Key Stages of the National Curriculum and has been divided into four sections, based on age and skill development, to create a clear path for staff and pupils to follow.

At all stages badminton is presented as a sport offering great fun. As the child gets older the more competitive instincts are introduced.

Equipment and resources

Five different sizes and standard of racket, exclusive to the BAofE, are offered, ranging from the BISI Mini used by juniors aged under 6 to BISI Graphite for the older and more skilful players.

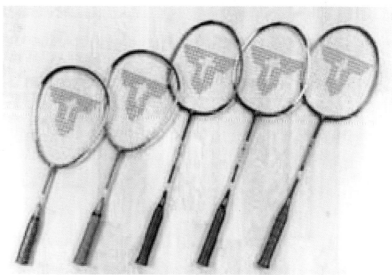

Key Stages for all

BISI 1

At BISI 1 youngsters under 6 years old get involved in a series of fun activities which can be delivered by parents, teachers, child-care workers or suitably qualified staff. The skills developed at this early level are fun-based and improve hand-eye co-ordination, depth perception and spatial awareness, providing a good introduction to a range of similar sports.

BISI 2

BISI 2 is for children between 7 and 10 and expands on the skills learned in the first stage. The emphasis shifts more on to badminton, but it is still relevant for other racket and ball sports. Within BISI 2 children can also start working towards a series of awards by achieving a set of required standards.

BISI 3

BISI 3 takes the programme a stage further and is suitable for 11–14 year olds. The focus is on badminton, with students playing competitive games. Pupils are encouraged to obtain higher standards of the award scheme.

BISI 4

BISI 4 can be tailored to fit with GCSE PE courses for students over 14. It aims to extend physical skills in order to reach a good level of badminton. The final stage also introduces the organisational aspects of the sport, ranging from coaching to running a club.

Progressive awards for pupils

Throughout all the Stages there is no testing – students are appraised by their peers and through self-assessment.

What do schools get?

Schools can obtain detailed and easy-to-follow Resource Cards for lesson planning and training for teachers is available from the BAofE. BISI is also part of the sports coach UK 'Coaching for Teachers' programme. A wide range of badminton-related resources is also available.

How does BISI fit in with other initiatives?

The BISI scheme has been very well received and is now in use in many schools throughout the country and is part of the Active Schools programme. BISI 1 complements Sport England's TOP play scheme and the remaining BISI stages work alongside the TOP Sport initiative.

What to do next

For more information including an order form and price list you can contact: The Development Department at the Badminton Association of England (*see* page 45 for details) or e-mail: BISI@baofe.co.uk

43

Badminton for the disabled

General information

Badminton has become a popular game among people with disabilities and there are a number of special coaching courses available. In response to this increase in popularity, the rules of the game have been amended to account for semi-ambulant and non-ambulant players. These adaptations can be found in the *Laws of Badminton*.

Badminton is administered worldwide by the International Badminton Federation (IBF). It has in excess of 142 member nations, which makes it one of the largest sporting bodies in the world. It is responsible for the management of the world team championships for men and women who compete for the Thomas Cup and the Uber Cup respectively.

For further information contact the Badminton Association of England, National Badminton Centre, Bradwell Road, Loughton Lodge, Milton Keynes, Bucks MK8 9LA.
Tel: 01908 268400
Fax: 01908 268412
E-mail: enquiries@baofe.co.uk
Website: www.baofe.co.uk

Questions and answers on the laws

Questions

1 A shuttle which falls on a line is held to fall within the part of the court bounded by that line. In taking up positions for serving or receiving within the appropriate half-court, does this same provision apply to your feet?

2 Must the shuttle when actually hit by the server be over the area defined as the half-court from which the service is due to be delivered?

3 The area within which the server must stand is clearly defined. Must the server's partner stand within the opposite half-court?

4 What is the correct decision covering a service which touches the top of the net and is obviously going to be a fault, but before it hits the floor it is intercepted by some part of the receiver's clothing?

5 In a doubles match the side which wins one game must commence serving in the next game. Which partner has to do this?

6 If in serving, you completely miss contacting the shuttle for some unaccountable reason, is this a fault?

7 The receiver's position is clearly defined as being within the diagonally opposite half-court to that of the server. How long must he stay there?

8 Are there any limitations on the position of the receiver's partner?

9 Once the service is delivered, what limitations are there on the positions of the players of each doubles pair?

10 If, in a doubles game, one of the players commences in the right half-court, he should obviously be in the same half-court whenever his side has scored an even number of points. Supposing, later on during the game, it is discovered that he is in the wrong half-court, should he and his partner immediately change sides?

11 Supposing you are not quite ready to receive the serve when it is delivered, but nevertheless make an attempt to return it, may you claim a 'let' because you were not ready?

12 What is the decision if the shuttle touches the roof in play?

13 What is the decision if the shuttle is deflected by a girder overhead?

14 What happens if a shuttle, after just passing over the net, is caught by the feathers on the tape or mesh of the net and remains suspended there?

15 In making a stroke a player hits the shuttle very cleanly, and with only one actual contact between racket and shuttle, on the frame of the racket. Is this a fair shot?

16 A shuttle is falling only just over the net, and may indeed actually drop on to the tape. May you lean over the net slightly with your racket in order to return it?

17 It is sometimes difficult to judge whether a shuttle will fall in or out of court, and therefore a player may prefer to return it. He does so and hits it round the post clearly below the level of the top of the net, but it falls on the line. Is this a fair shot or not?

18 When there is no umpire, should a player call his own faults, or should he wait for the opponents to claim them?

19 May a player call to his partner to take a shuttle or leave it because it may be going out of court?

Answers

1 No. A foot on the line is held to be outside the service court, and it is therefore a fault (Laws 9.1.2 and 9.2).

2 No. The restrictions from where the service shall be delivered are imposed only on the player's feet and there is no objection to his leaning, or extending his racket, beyond the lines (Law 9).

3 No. He may stand where he likes provided that he does not unsight the receiver. The receiver is entitled to a clear and uninterrupted view of the shuttle (Law 9.7).

4 A fault against the receiver, and the server wins the point (Law 13.2.5).

5 Either partner may serve, but he must do so from the right-hand court (Laws 11.9 and 11.5).

6 Yes (Law 9.3).

7 Some part of both of his feet must remain in contact with the surface of the court, in a stationary position, from the start of the service (Law 9.4), until the shuttle is actually struck by the server. Once the service has been delivered, he may, however, step beyond the limits of the half-court to return it (Law 9.1.3).

8 There are no restrictions at all provided that he does not unsight the server in any way (Law 9.7).

9 The only limitations are that they must not prevent an opponent from making a legal stroke where the shuttle is followed over the net (Law 13.4.4) and they must not invade the opponents' court over or under the net with racket or person such that an opponent is obstructed or distracted (Laws 13.4.2 and 13.4.3).

10 No. If the mistake is not discovered at once, they should remain where they are and carry on as if there had been no mistake (Law 12.2).

11 No. A player is deemed to be ready if an attempt is made to return the shuttle. If you are not ready, you should make no attempt to play the shuttle (Law 9.5).

12 It is a fault (Law 13.2.4). If you could claim a 'let' for hitting the roof you might deliberately hit it whenever you were in difficulties. In special circumstances, however, it may be a 'let' under local by-laws.

13 You should enquire about this prior to play. Law 13.2.6 gives the local badminton authority power to make a by-law concerning such a matter.

14 It counts as a 'let' except during service (Law 14.1.3).

15 Yes. It is a fair shot. The law was altered in 1963.

16 No. That would be invasion of your opponents' court. You must wait until the shuttle has passed over the net, but in making your stroke you may follow through with your racket over the net provided that at the moment of contact the shuttle is on your side (Law 13.3).

17 It is a fair shot.

18 A player should always call his own faults, and he should call them immediately. Where, however, there is an umpire, it will be his duty to call them.

19 Certainly. The two players form a team, and they may assist each other how they like. On no account, however, should any spectator give any advice during play.

Index